First published in the United States by
Larousse & Co., Inc.
572 Fifth Avenue
New York, N.Y. 10036
1978

Reprinted 1981

First published in Denmark by
Gyldendal in 1978 as *Askepot*

Illustrations Copyright © 1978 Svend Otto S
English Translation Copyright © 1978 Anne Rogers

ISBN 0-88332-093-2

Library of Congress Catalog Card No. 78-50997

Printed in Denmark

GRIMM
Cinderella

Illustrated by Svend Otto S.

Translated by Anne Rogers

Larousse & Co., Inc. *New York*

There was once a rich man whose wife was ill. She knew she was dying, so she called her only daughter to her bedside. "Always be good, dear child, and God will look after you," she said. Then she closed her eyes and died.

The girl did as she was told. Every day she went to her mother's grave and wept. Winter came and covered the grave with a white blanket of snow, and when the spring sun was warm enough to melt it, her father married again.

His new wife already had two daughters. They were
beautiful but wicked and treated their step-sister cruelly.

"The silly goose wants to eat with us," they said. "She
must earn her keep. Get out, kitchen-maid!"

They took away her fine shoes and clothes and made her
put on clogs and an old grey dress. "Just look at her, the grand
princess—isn't she gorgeous?" they jeered, pushing her into
the kitchen.

They made her do all the heavy work from dawn to dusk. She fetched water, made the fires, cooked and washed. Her step-sisters thought of every way they could to tease and torment her. They even threw lentils into the ashes and told her to pick them out again.

By the end of the day she was very tired, but they would not let her lie down in bed. She had to sleep on the hearth in the cinders. So she came to be called Cinderella.

One day her father was going to the town. He asked his
two step-daughters what he should bring back for them.
"Fine clothes," said one. "Pearls and precious stones," said
the other. "And you, Cinderella, what would you like?" "A
twig—the first that brushes against your hat on the way
home; please break it off for me."

So he bought fine clothes, pearls and precious stones for his
step-daughters. As he rode home a hazel twig brushed his hat

off. He cut it from the branch and took it with him. He gave his step-daughters all they had asked for, and the hazel twig to Cinderella. She thanked him and went out to her mother's grave, where she planted the twig. It grew into a beautiful tree. Three times a day Cinderella stood under it, weeping and praying. One morning a white bird came and perched on the tree and listened to her prayers. If she wished for something, the bird threw down to her whatever she desired.

Now the king wanted his son to choose a bride, so he invited all the beautiful young women in the country to a wedding feast lasting three days. The two step-sisters were overjoyed when their invitation came, and they kept Cinderella busier than ever. "Brush our hair, clean our shoes

and get our best clothes ready—we are going to the wedding feast at the king's palace."

With tears in her eyes Cinderella did as she was told. She longed to go to the ball, and asked her step-mother if she could go too. "You? You're dusty and dirty, you have neither fine clothes nor shoes, yet you want to go to the ball!" But Cinderella begged and pleaded, till at last she said, "Very well. I've thrown a bowlful of lentils into the ashes. If you've picked them out again in two hours' time, you can go too."

The girl went out to the garden and called: "Gentle doves, turtle doves, how can I pick up all those lentils? Come with all the birds of the air and help me, please,

the good ones put into my bowl,
the bad ones you can swallow whole.''
Two white doves flew in through the kitchen window. All
the birds of the air followed and pecked busily among the
ashes. It took them an hour to finish picking out the lentils
and putting the good ones in the bowl. Then they all flew
away.

Cinderella took the full bowl to her step-mother. ''May I
go to the ball now?'' she asked. ''No,'' said her step-mother,

"you can't dance and you have no proper clothes. People
would only laugh at you."

Cinderella burst into tears. "You must pick out two bowls
of lentils from the ashes in one hour," said her step-mother.
"If you do that, you may go to the ball." She thought the girl
could not possibly finish the task in an hour.

She threw the lentils into the ashes and Cinderella went
out to the garden, calling: "Gentle doves, turtle doves and all
the birds of the air, come and help me pick up the lentils,

        the good ones put into each bowl,
        the bad ones you can swallow whole."

Two white doves flew in through the kitchen window, then
the turtle doves and all the birds of the air came fluttering in
and pecked busily among the ashes. Half an hour later they
had finished and flown away.

Cinderella ran to her step-mother and showed her the two bowls full of lentils. She felt sure that she could now go to the ball.

"It's no good—you can't go," said her step-mother. "You have no clothes and you don't know how to dance. We'd be ashamed of you." She turned and hurried away with her two disdainful daughters.

Now that she was alone, Cinderella went to her mother's grave under the tree and said:
"Shake and shiver, hazel tree,
Throw gold and silver down to me."
The bird threw down a dress made of gold and silver, and

a pair of satin slippers embroidered with silver, too. She dressed very quickly and in no time at all she arrived at the palace. Her sisters did not recognize her in her new splendour. They thought she must be some unknown princess. They certainly didn't guess it was Cinderella, whom they had last seen looking for lentils in the ashes.

The king's son asked her to dance with him. He would not dance with anyone else. If another man asked her, the prince said, "She is my partner."

When evening came she got ready to go home. "I will go with you," the prince said. He wanted to see where she lived and who her family were.

But she ran away from him and hid in the dove-cote.
The prince waited till Cinderella's father came home.
"There's a strange girl hiding in your dove-cote," the prince
told him. "That must be Cinderella," thought her father. He
called for an axe and chopped down the dove-cote; there was
nobody in it.

They went into the house. There was Cinderella in her dirty clothes asleep on the hearth. An oil lamp burned brightly in the chimney. She had jumped out of the back of the dove-cote and run to the hazel tree, taken off her fine clothes and left them on the grave for the bird to take away. Then she ran indoors in her old grey dress and lay down on the hearth.

Next day, all the others set off for the wedding feast again and Cinderella was left alone. She went to the hazel tree and said:

"Shake and shiver, hazel tree,
Throw gold and silver down to me."

The bird threw down an even more splendid dress than before.

When Cinderella appeared at the ball, everyone marvelled at her beauty. The prince was waiting for her. He took her hand and danced with her and nobody else. If other men wanted to dance with her, he said, "She is my partner."

When evening came she tried to slip away. The prince

followed her to see where she lived, but she ran ahead to the
garden behind the house. In the garden was a big tree laden
with ripe pears. As the prince stood looking at it, Cinderella
ran up its branches as nimbly as a squirrel and he lost sight of
her. So he waited till her father came home.

"The mysterious girl has vanished," said the prince. "I
think she climbed up the pear tree."

"That must be Cinderella," her father thought to himself.
He called for an axe and chopped down the tree, but there
was nobody in it. They went into the kitchen. Cinderella was
lying on the hearth as before, fast asleep. She had jumped
down from the other side of the tree, given the fine clothes
back to the bird and put her old grey dress on again.

Next day, as soon as the others were out of the house, Cinderella went to her mother's grave and said for the third time:

> "Shake and shiver, hazel tree,
> Throw gold and silver down to me."

The bird threw down an even more magnificent dress than before—nobody had ever had anything like it—and the slippers were of pure gold. When Cinderella arrived at the wedding feast, everyone was dumbfounded. The prince danced only with her, and if other men came near, he said, "She is my partner."

When evening came, Cinderella tried to go home
unnoticed. The prince wanted to go with her, but she slipped
away so quickly that he lost sight of her.

But he had played a trick on her; the whole staircase had
been smeared with tar. As she ran away her left slipper came
off and stuck to the stair. The prince lifted up the dainty little
shoe—it was made of pure gold.

Next day he went to Cinderella's father and said, "I will marry nobody but the girl whose foot this shoe fits."

The step-sisters were overjoyed to hear this, for they both had elegant feet. First the elder girl took the shoe and went inside to try it on while her mother watched. But her foot was too long; she could not get her big toe in. Her mother handed her a knife saying: "Cut your toe off; when you're a queen you won't need to walk."

The girl chopped off her toe and squeezed her foot into the shoe. She pretended she was not in pain and went out to the

prince. He lifted her up on to his horse and rode away to
make her his bride.

They had to pass the grave. Two doves were sitting on the
hazel tree, calling to the prince:

"Coo-co-ri-coo! This won't do!
There's blood in the shoe.
Home you must ride
To find your true bride."

The prince looked at the girl's foot and saw the blood on it.
He turned his horse and took the girl home. He said she was
the wrong one—the other sister must try on the shoe.

So the younger step-sister went inside and tried it on. She managed to get her toes into the slipper, but her heel would not go in. So her mother gave her a knife, saying, "Cut a bit of your heel off; when you're a queen you won't need to walk."

The girl cut a bit off her heel and squeezed her foot into the shoe. Pretending it did not hurt, she went out to the prince. He lifted her on to his horse and rode away to make her his bride.

As they went past the grave, two doves were sitting on the hazel tree, calling:

> "Coo-co-ri-coo! This won't do!
> There's blood in the shoe.
> Home you must ride
> To find your true bride."

The prince bent down and saw that the girl's shoe was full of blood and her white stockings were turning red. So he took her home. "This is not the right one either," he said.

"Haven't you another daughter?" "No," said the man.
"There's only my first wife's child, Cinderella, and she's a
poor little thing. She couldn't possibly be your bride."

The prince said, "Bring her here." But the step-mother
refused: "She's much too dirty—not fit to be seen."

But he insisted, and Cinderella was sent for. First she
washed her hands and face, then ran and curtseyed to the
prince, who gave her the golden slipper. She sat on a stool,
took off her heavy clogs and put on the slipper. It fitted
perfectly, as though it had been made for her. She stood up
and the prince looked into her face. He recognized the lovely
girl he had danced with, and called out, "This is my true
bride!"

The step-mother and her two daughters went pale with
anger; but he took Cinderella on his horse and they rode
away. As they passed the hazel tree the two white doves
called:

> "Coo-co-ri-coo!
> No blood in the shoe.
> To the king you must ride,
> For you've found your true bride."

Then the doves flew down and settled on Cinderella's shoulders, one on each side.

On Cinderella's wedding day her step-sisters wanted to share in her new glory. They joined the bridal procession, one on each side. But the doves punished them both for their wickedness and pecked out their eyes, so they were blind for the rest of their lives.